MW01231156

Unleash and Soar

Start Today Living Boldly and Beyond Limits

Tina Moore Brown

Unleash and Soar
Copyright 2017 TMB Publishing
All Rights Reserved

Published by TMB Publishing
Raleigh, North Carolina

Printed in the United States of America.
No part of this book may be reproduced, stored in a retrieval system, or transmitted in any form or by any means, electronic, mechanical, including photocopying, recording, or otherwise, without the written permission of the publisher/authors.

ISBN-13: 978-1543291865
ISBN-10: 1543291864

For booking information contact:
Tina Moore Brown
Phone: 919.391.0313
Email:tmb@tinamoorebrown.com
Website: **www.TinaMooreBrown.com**

Discounts on this book are available for bulk purchases.
Contact us for prices.

~

This book is dedicated to
the woman I most admire.
She is the strongest woman I know
and is a survivor in every sense of the word.
She is a person who never stops soaring.
She is my mother,
Aileen Powell Moore

Thank you for showing me how to soar.

~

Table of Contents

INTRODUCTION..7

HOW TO USE THIS BOOK.........................10

YOU ARE ON THE RIGHT TRACK................13

TAKE YOUR TIME.....................................16

WHAT'S HOLDING YOU BACK?.................19

LET IT GO..22

DECISIONS, DECISIONS..........................24

CONFIDENCE IS KEY...............................27

WHATEVER IT IS, FIX IT...........................30

STAY READY...32

BECOME UNBREAKABLE.........................35

YOUR COMFORT ZONE IS KILLING YOU...........39

DON'T TAKE IT PERSONALLY.........................42

TAKE THE RAW STUFF..................................46

JUST SAY IT...48

WE'VE BEEN WAITING ON YOU.....................51

GET RID OF IT...53

DESTROY THAT BOX......................................55

THIS TOO SHALL PASS...................................58

OPPOSITION...61

PERCEPTION IS EVERYTHING.........................64

DREAM AGAIN...67

IT'S ALREADY IN YOU.....................................70

TIME KEEPS ON TICKING...............................73

RELAX...76

STAND...79

REMAIN FLEXIBLE..82

MOVE SOMETHING..84

CLOSE THE DOOR BEHIND YOU....................87

TAKE CONTROL OF YOUR LIFE.....................89

YOU ARE AN ORIGINAL. STOP FIGHTING IT...91

TRUST IN GOD...93

ACKNOWLEDGEMENTS..................................94

ABOUT THE AUTHOR....................................96

INTRODUCTION

Betrayal. Fear. Depression. Failure. Broken relationships. Divorce. Eviction. Abandonment. I'd experienced it all before the age of 40. If you think for one minute that the woman who authored this book is perfect I hate to disappoint you. I'm far from perfect but even further from defeat. Yes, I've experienced all the things above but none of them kept me from pushing forward. None of them.

All my life I've had the desire to see people excel. I cheer for the underdog because I've been the underdog. I can relate to those who weren't or didn't feel good about themselves, pretty or popular. I wanted to see others excel because deep down I had this gnawing feeling that I would succeed and surmount the odds. It was buried under layers of 'stuff' but it still existed. Circumstances and situations would try to push that feeling down but it never went away.

After divorce, foreclosure, a lot of gossiping from those around me I found myself at the lowest point in my life … and guess what? The desire to excel was still inside me. Yes, I had to uncover it from all of life's debris and as miniscule as it may have appeared it still existed. I so badly wanted to snap my fingers and change my life. I wanted to live in the midst of that "feeling to excel"; however, that feeling never died no matter how rocky life got I knew it must be my destiny to live boldly and beyond limits.

Just three years later my life changed drastically and the dreams I dreamt became my reality. My desire to excel never died and neither did my desire to see others excel; that is why you are reading this book. It was one thing for my life to turn around but what about yours? Why should you remain where you are when I can show you the way out?

My desire is for you to learn how to live boldly even when you are faced with tough circumstances. This book is dedicated to that goal. While you read this book be reminded of the underdog. Everyone counts the underdog out except the underdog. If there is something inside telling you that you can soar, it's possible. Follow me and together we can get you from where you are to where you have dreamt of being. What took me years may take you months. I didn't have an Unleash and Soar book to guide me through … just a pen and a pad wet with a lot of tears.

Unleash and Soar is part of me fulfilling my destiny and now I want to help you get up and get started fulfilling yours. My path to get here as an author wasn't an easy one and I'd guess yours hasn't been so either. Anyone who purchases this book must have a gnawing inside for more and is fully aware that more doesn't just walk up and sit in your lap. You must work for more. Chase after more and long for more. I'm not talking about more friends, Facebook likes, Twitter followers or pats on the back. I'm talking about more of your destiny being revealed to you. Contrary to what I used to think you just aren't handed a clear picture of your destination. People lead you to believe they always knew what they were called or created to do or be and they just stepped out and evolved; supposedly, but no. I've learned that this journey of life has many detours, pit stops, setbacks and bumps in the road but they all are necessary to shape you into who you are becoming. I like to look at it like this. Your destiny was ready for you the day you were born, but you were in no shape or form ready. It is taking everything you go through on your way to your destiny to ensure you and your destiny are ready for each other. The last thing you want is to reach it and not be ready.

It doesn't matter what your life looks like right now. It doesn't matter how many times you've attempted to change. It doesn't even matter if you don't have support from family or friends. What matters is that somewhere, deep down inside, you have a desire for more. If you do, take my hand and let's unleash your potential so you can begin to soar! The sky is waiting.

HOW TO USE THIS BOOK

If you ask me, we are all born with greatness deposited inside of us. Yes, greatness. Not okay-ness or regular-ness but greatness. If we aren't why would we exist? I refuse to believe that there are only certain people destined for greatness and the rest of us are just fillers here to give them an audience. Each of us has a destiny to fulfill and a space and time to soar. All of us! Yes, that includes you. I'd bet that's the very reason you're reading this book today.

There are times in all our lives when we need to remind ourselves to live boldly and beyond limits. Situations will arise and cause us to second guess ourselves and our abilities. If the latter persists you notice you are living within limits and boundaries and you'll wonder how it happened. For some it's the opinions of others that keep us from soaring. For others it's our own thoughts, memories and feelings that create the limits we see in life. Each chapter speaks to a different area in your life. Feel free to read straight through the book and glean from it. You may want to find the section that hits home with you right now and park there for a moment allowing it to speak to you until you've unleashed and begun to soar. At the end of each chapter you will find affirmations, something to unleash and space for you to elaborate on how you will soar.

AFFIRMATIONS

Your words matter. Period. Where do those words you speak every day come from? Your thoughts. You probably haven't paid much attention to your thoughts lately. Maybe they just pop up and you respond. I began believing in the power of affirmations or confessions in 1998. I had returned from vacation to Cancun, Mexico to find out my mother had to have quadruple by-pass surgery. My mother is the strongest person I know and I never saw her unable to care for herself before in my life. During the weeks of recuperation, she would verbally confess *"weakness go, strength come."* I witnessed firsthand her road to recovery and attributed it with her daily confessions.

You may not be aware of it but the words you use define you. They come from your underlying beliefs about yourself. If you aren't aware of the power of your words let's look at it. Your words create your reality and your words come from the thoughts you think. Words that are positive build you up and words that are negative tear you down. It's simple and plain. In this book, I'll help you create the results you are looking for by thinking the right thoughts. Let's go from thinking positive thoughts to speaking words to having positive experiences. At the end of each chapter you'll find an affirmation to repeat because you can't unleash or soar until you've changed your words and thoughts around a matter.

UNLEASH

The word **unleash** means to be released or become unrestrained. There are sometimes areas in our lives that have us bound. Think about it. Have you been trying to shake procrastination for years? Are you known for arriving late? Does a quick temper have a hold on you? These are all things we need to be released from. Each chapter has a topic and as we just learned an affirmation. The unleash section allows you to pin point a specific area that has a grip on you. It allows you to put a finger on one thing that needs work.

SOAR

The word *soar* means to increase rapidly above the usual level. Once we upgrade our thinking with affirmations and identify what's been holding us down it's time to determine ways we can rise above our present circumstances. At the end of each chapter I have provided space for notes on how to determine how you will soar!

YOU ARE ON THE RIGHT TRACK

In life, we are taught to make plans. As children, adults ask us what we want to be when we grow up. As teens, we decide if college will be our next step after high school and soon the application process begins. As college freshmen, we must decide on a major. We plan our futures as best as we can and creating a road map for life at an early age can be exciting. "By 25 years old I'll be on my own with a college degree ... by 30 I'll be married .... by 33 I'll have a child .... I'll own my own business by 35 and retire early by 50." If your life fell in line with the plans you made as a young adult I'd like to issue you a big congratulation! Most us have worn out the erasers on our pencils from editing our plans so much.

Life has a way of making turns you never see coming. A marriage may end in divorce. The child you hoped to have may be harder to conceive than you'd planned and oftentimes with difficulties come a lot of unexpected issues. Solutions take time and now your life's timeline seems way off track. Sometimes the twists and turns life takes aren't all bad ones, just ones we hadn't expected. I have a friend named Mary and she always thought she'd be a lawyer. She attended college and in her sophomore year she fell in love with psychology. For as long as she could remember she loved helping people work through their problems. After 15 years of working in corporate America, Mary left a job she hated and became life coach. Mary's path to discover her passion wasn't a straight line from college to life coach and that's true for many of us. Mary's issue was that she thought she would be much further along in life than she was. Have you ever had that feeling?

News flash – it hasn't taken you too long. You are right on track. You don't understand that because you can't see your entire path from where you are. You can only see where you've been and where you are now. Sometimes it's hard to pin point where you are going - especially when you are embarking upon unfamiliar territory. But God knows your end from your beginning which means He is the only One who knows exactly where you are on the path of life. Most of us are trying to figure out when will we reach the place called THERE ... when will we get IT. I don't think we ever get THERE or get IT because we continue to learn and evolve and think we should be THERE by now. What we don't realize is that during the journey we've gained experiences. We've matured and we now see things from several different perspectives and we can reach a wider audience than we were when we were younger and thought we were ready. You're not behind. Don't get fearful and start scrambling thinking you must throw something together because those around you are excelling. Step back to look at the entire picture of your life. See how your journey has led you to where you are today. Then you will really see what you must offer the world.

AFFIRMATION

I press forward because I believe in my path.

I feel motivated because I am moving in the direction of my dreams.

New opportunities are showing up for me daily.

UNLEASH

Release the need to spend time reliving your past. Regret has no place in your life. Move forward daily and expect wonderful things to happen to you and for you.

SOAR

_____

_____

_____

_____

_____

_____

TAKE YOUR TIME

It is difficult to be great when you are overwhelmed. Work, family, church, children, school, volunteering and supporting your friends. There are only 24 hours in everyone's day and no one gets extra time no matter how badly we need it. If you are stretched to the max it may be time to re-evaluate your priorities and change the way you distribute your time.

Each week we have 168 hours allocated. You are asleep for about 56 of those (if you need eight hours a night like me), so we are left with 112 hours. If you are not careful you can waste more time than you are aware. One of my favorite quotes is *"if you fail to plan you plan to fail"* by Benjamin Franklin. If we're going to take advice from anyone shouldn't it be someone who invented bifocal glasses, discovered electricity and set up the US colonies or the first national communications network? A week that you fail to plan is seven days of organized chaos. Take one week and set and live by your schedule and you too will be quoting dear old Ben.

Here's how I plan to succeed each week instead of planning to fail. On Saturday, I set aside about an hour to get comfy with my pen, paper and calendar. I create a master TO GET ACCOMPLISHED list for the next seven days. Everything I can think of I put it on my calendar. I schedule my grocery trips, identify the days I'll do laundry and even my exercise plan for the week. Think of yourself as the CEO of a Fortune 500 company and schedule your time wisely. Once you've created your weekly to do list pull from it nightly to create a to do list for the following day. Each day you rise, your to do list awaits you. That's one less thing you must do each morning. If you're a mom of a few school aged kids you'll thank me for that tip because morning time is precious. Anyone who struggles with creating a routine that works each morning should consider reading "What the Most Successful People Do Before Breakfast" by Laura Vanderkam.

Once you experience the benefits of creating a weekly schedule and how easily you'll take your time back. YOU are the guard over every hour, minute and second in your life. Refuse to haphazardly give your time away. Schedule it, stick to your schedule and be a more productive you. That's how you prepare for success!

AFFIRMATION

I am a good steward of my time because I realize how precious it is.

Planning, scheduling and managing my time is important to me because I value in the time I've been given.

UNLEASH

Let go of the need to procrastinate. Putting off undesirable tasks for later causes stress and prolongs the inevitable. Tackle situations and project head on with the confidence of knowing that the wonderful feeling of completion awaits you.

SOAR

_____

_____

_____

_____

_____

_____

WHAT'S HOLDING YOU BACK?

There is nothing worse than feeling like you want to progress in life but you can't. You almost feel as though your feet are glued to the ground. It is usually in those times that it seems like everyone around you is moving forward at high speed. I'm not talking about being in a rut. See, a rut is something that you can change like your hairstyle and lipstick color. You can snap out of a rut but bondage is something different. Bondage is like something that has a hold on you. You don't have it, it has you.

Bondage looks like staying in an unhealthy relationship because you are afraid of being alone. Sometimes we choose relationships for the wrong reasons. I certainly know what it is to find myself in love with someone who doesn't have my best interest at heart. In my 20's I fell in love with a "bad guy". You know the type ... a street guy that's flashy, stylish, has major swag and the money to match. For years I held on to a piece of a relationship because I loved how I felt being around him, but in the back of my mind I knew I deserved more. After being disrespected countless times and turning a blind eye and deaf ear to things I remember sitting on the couch in my apartment asking God to help me end this ... and He did. I knew the expiration date had long passed on the relationship but I was holding on to convenience and it was making me sick. Sick of not being first, sick of the lies, sick of wanting better, sick of needing to be loved like I knew I should. After seven years I walked away and never looked back.

Bondage looks like allowing fear to keep you in a job you hate instead of moving closer to starting your own business. After working in corporate America for seven years I said, "I QUIT". Why? I absolutely hated it. The skills I learned helped me as an entrepreneur and I'm grateful for the things I learned and people I met while I was there, but I knew it wasn't where I belonged. Each morning I woke up felt like torture. I wasn't popping up out of bed excited about what the day may bring. I was dreading getting dressed and sitting behind a desk for eight hours pushing paper and manipulating spreadsheets. I left and started a dance studio and yes, each morning I popped out of bed because I was doing what I was built to do. Freedom feels so good!

Bondage looks like avoiding family members during holidays because you refuse to forgive them. Bondage looks like continuing to carry around excessive body fat because you refuse to make the necessary changes to get healthy. Bondage is continuing to dismiss that business idea because you have chained yourself to your family's to do list day in and day out and they cannot (more like refuse) to live without you catering to their every need.

My question to you is "what's holding you back from living the life you thought you'd be living"?

We all have an idea of where we'll be by this point in life or by that stage in life. If your response to that question sounds anything like an excuse, find another response. You've been given one life here on earth and if you haven't noticed let me inform you that it's too precious to waste. You deserve to live the life you dreamed. How do you get from where you are to where you desire to be? The first step is to remove thoughts that keep you bound to where you are and hold you back from success. The "I can't", "I'm too old", "I don't have enough money". Excuses wrap around your mind and paralyze any thoughts of moving forward. Wiggle free from the words, situations and hurts that have kept you tied up and unable to move forward. You deserve to soar!

AFFIRMATION

My thoughts are filled with positivity and my life is plentiful with prosperity.
I see every challenge through.
I always win.

UNLEASH

Let go of the fear that keeps you from moving forward. Let the thing you desire grow larger in your mind than fear.

SOAR

_____

_____

_____

_____

_____

LET IT GO

End. Finish. Terminate. Close. Stop. If I give you 10 minutes I believe you can come up with at least 10 things that no longer serve you but are still showing up in your life. We sometimes tend to carry what we no longer need. When we do we have less room to receive what is new and next in our lives and we wonder why we sometimes feel 'stuck'. It may be time to release what no longer serves you in this season.

At the end of each meal you set aside your remains and immediately dispose of them. Why? If you walk around with ends of your sandwich bread, an apple core and empty bottles of water (1) you'd look crazy to the rest of the world, (2) you'd accumulate a lot of junk by the end of the day and (3) well, to be frank, you'd stink. When it comes to dining we are aware of the need to take in what we need and dispose of rest. I think it would be a great idea to adopt this way of thinking in life as well.

Take this opportunity to let go of some things that just don't belong in your life any longer. Do you need to bring closure to a situation? Maybe you need to wave goodbye to an old way of thinking. Are your friendships healthy? Make this part of your daily routine just as it is your dining experience. Keep what you need and let go of what doesn't serve you.

AFFIRMATION

I quickly release what no longer serves me.
I can let go of negative people, places and things.
I daily assess my load and I am constantly making it lighter.

UNLEASH

Release what no longer serves you. Refuse to be the 'bag lady' that hold on unimportant thoughts, emotions, situations or experiences and make room for more.

SOAR

_____

_____

_____

_____

_____

DECISIONS, DECISIONS

How is your mind doing today? Have you checked in with it lately? We give attention to our weight, our skin, our hair but what about the condition of your mind? Your thinking plays a key role in where you are and how quickly you will get where you desire to go in life.

Elevation requires a shift in thinking. Once you shift your mindset, your life begins to soar. Changing the way, you approach life will set you on another path because you can only go as high as your thoughts take you. It doesn't matter if you quote the entire Bible over your life, if you don't change the way you THINK those scriptures are mere words that will never take on life.

Today, make the decision to change your self-talk. Self-talk occurs every day. It is the conversation you have with yourself about yourself. *"I don't think I'll ever get through this"*, *"I'm not strong enough to get out of this"*, *"things never work out for me"*. I came across a quote while preparing for one of my Confidence is Key conference calls. It says, *"when you doubt your power you give power to your doubt."* Do you agree?

Come to a place where you believe that what's inside of you *is* good enough. An acorn seed, as small as it is it produces a full-blown tree. The seed already has all it needs to become a tree inside. Inside of you is everything you need to become who you are at your highest level. Why waste valuable time looking outside of yourself to find what's already inside of you?

Either fully believe in yourself or allow doubt to take over. You don't need a reason to believe in yourself – just do it. Again, you have two choices. Which will you choose? Make the decision to believe in yourself today and never look back.

AFFIRMATION

I am good enough.
I am valuable.
I am perfect just as I am.

UNLEASH

Let go of the belief that you aren't good enough. Decide to acknowledge your value and unleash your inner confidence!

SOAR

_____

_____

_____

_____

_____

CONFIDENCE IS KEY

Without healthy self- esteem, many areas of your life will suffer. If you struggle with believing in yourself then starting a business sounds like a crazy idea. If you are unsure of your identity then standing out and creating a brand for yourself is impossible. If you are looking outside of yourself for worth it is safe to say a new relationship is doomed from the start. To function properly and grow in life confidence is key.

Meet Ann. Ann is from a small town and moved to a big city not too long ago. Her parents never made her feel valuable, so she never really saw herself as worthy of love. One Sunday she stumbled upon a church that took her in and showered her with love and Ann finally felt a sense of belonging. Although she found a space where she fit there was still an emptiness inside. Although Ann developed a wonderful relationship with God she still struggled with not feeling good enough, enough or deeply loved. Ann discovered my Confidence is Key conference calls and coaching sessions online and quickly registered. Within a matter of months Ann discovered the key to unlock doors that held her hostage in her youth. She already knew God loved her and the coaching sessions gave her insight on why she hadn't loved herself. Ann had mimicked the actions of her family members. They overlooked her value and she did as well. Ann made a conscious decision to take the time to love and believe in herself again. She knew God saw her as forgiven, redeemed and as a conqueror and now it was time to view herself through the lenses of her Savior. The once shy, quiet and soft spoken young lady blossomed into a strong, powerful, confident woman all because she found her confidence.

Many people hear the word confidence and immediately think of arrogance. I ask that you not swing so far to the left and let's look at the word. Confidence has many definitions and one is *"a feeling of self-assurance arising from one's appreciation of one's own abilities or qualities."* Arrogance means *"an attitude of superiority manifested in an overbearing manner or in presumptuous claims or assumptions."* Do you see the difference? I know of people who are afraid of confidence because they think it is synonymous with arrogance and it is not. A famous quote from Marianne Williamson entitled Our Deepest Fear reads *"We are all meant to shine, as children do. We were born to make manifest the glory of God that is within us. It's not just in some of us; it's in everyone."* If our Creator made us in His image and we house His Holy Spirit how can we be worthless, useless, unlovable or empty?

AFFIRMATION

I am who God says I am.
My presence in the world matters.
I possess the qualities needed to be extremely successful.

UNLEASH

Identify areas where you have been playing small in life.
Make the decision to come out of the background and take
center stage in your own life. There is no reward for playing
small or shrinking. Unleash your inner confidence and stand
tall knowing that you walk this earth for a reason and you
have a contribution to make to the world.

SOAR

_____

_____

_____

_____

_____

_____

WHATEVER IT IS, FIX IT

Meet Janet. At one point in Janet's life she was a real go-getter. She was a track star in high school, a scholar and fun to be around. Janet landed an excellent job and somehow her work became her life. She no longer found time for social activities, exercise or having fun. Janet's stressful job left her mentally and physically drained at the end of each day. When she looked in the mirror she no longer saw the old Janet - slender, fit, bright smile. She saw a pudgy, middle-aged woman who wore the stress of life like a heavy coat. Deep down she wanted her old self back but unfortunately her excuses kept her from making the necessary changes.

Your blood pressure. Your attitude. The need to procrastinate. Blaming others. Not keeping your word. Lack of follow through. Whatever stands between you and the best you that you could be ...address it. If you don't you'll continue to age but you won't grow. You will be an older person with the same old issues.

I have a friend who is an entrepreneur with a procrastination issue. Katie loses contracts, clients, business and money all because she refuses to correct her procrastination problem. Don't wait to fix it (*that's what procrastinators do, don't they*)?

You may be a wife with an overbearing attitude. You control your husband, your kids and everyone around you. If left unattended you will lose the respect of your kids, genuine affection from your husband and the company of any friends who refuse to put up with your ways. Don't wait. Fix it.

AFFIRMATION

My obstacles are moving out of my way; my path is carved towards greatness.
I make wise decisions.

UNLEASH

Identify the area that needs to be fixed. Where is the disconnect? What exactly needs to change? Time management? Poor diet? A bad relationship? It may take a moment to identify the root of your problem but once you do you can move towards change.

SOAR

_____

_____

_____

_____

_____

STAY READY

Have you ever carpooled with someone? If they ask you to be ready at a certain time it is in your best interest to be ready and waiting with your bags in tow. Being ready is the least you can do considering you are not doing the driving. On the other hand, if you are the driver and you've agreed to pick up a friend at 1pm how frustrating is it when you pull up on time and they stick their head out of the door motioning for you to come inside?

Ready for what you ask? There's an old saying that goes "*if you stay ready you never have to get ready.*" Yes, that's pretty much the truth. Why wait until you see your next big break or your next level to prepare for it? If you do you are too late. Opportunities are like unexpected guests. They sometimes show up unannounced. My mother keeps a clean house 24/7 and is never and I mean never caught off guard when company just drops by. She stays ready to receive guests. Are you always ready to receive the positive things life may send your way?

Preparation is key for a successful life. Look at it this way, if you are going to make a new dish you've never tried before for dinner you usually follow a recipe in a cookbook. The instructions clearly tell you how much prep time you'll need, gives you a list of ingredients and lets you know when you can expect it to be on your table.

There is no way you can just jump into creating a dish you've never made without the necessary prep work like grocery shopping, washing vegetables and cleaning your kitchen. Just as prep work is necessary for creating a spectacular meal the same is true with creating a spectacular life.

AFFIRMATION

I make smart, calculated plans for my future.
Every positive action I take accelerates my progress.
With a solid plan and belief in myself, there is nothing I
cannot accomplish.

UNLEASH

What areas in your life need improvement? Once you have
identified them create a plan on how you can grow using
very little effort (self-help books from the library, online
courses, coaching sessions, etc.).

SOAR

_____

_____

_____

_____

_____

BECOME UNBREAKABLE

Let no one, absolutely no one tear you down.

Remember the saying *"sticks and stones by break my bones but words will never hurt me?"* I think it was started by someone who was verbally abused and they used it as a mantra to feel better. Has anyone ever used words to hurt you? I've never been physically abused but I can say that the sting of hurtful words from someone you love can cut you deep. Because you didn't walk away with a black eye or bruises may cause the culprit to think that an apology isn't warranted because *"they were only words so get over it."* Well, it's not that simple!

People who are in your inner circle can hurt you the most. You've opened your heart and given parts of yourself that others never see only to turn around and get your heart crushed. It makes you want to crawl in bed and cry for days.

Wives if you've ever struggled with communication in your marriage you know it can be extremely frustrating when you feel you aren't being heard. To be talked down to, demeaned or treated like anything except his partner can leave you puzzled. Over time the sting of harmful words can make you like your partner less with each altercation until you are left numb and have completely shut off your emotions to stop the pain.

You are NOT what someone says you are.
Who are you?
You are the creation of the Most High!
You are made in the image of the King.
You are an original creation from head to toe.
You serve a purpose in this world.
You are valuable.

Dwelling on the pain only feeds it and anything you feed grows! Instead of replaying the conversations and experiences over and over in your head chose to build yourself up and speak positively about yourself repeatedly. Remember, anything you feed grows.

So, how do you heal from hurts? We all have them. Family hurts. Relationship hurts. Church hurts. It starts with forgiving yourself and acknowledging your part that led to the hurt. Maybe it's time to change how you approach situations. Maybe it's time to stop over extending yourself to people. Whatever your part is - because you do play a part - acknowledge it and forgive yourself. One of my pet peeves is talking with someone about an issue they are facing and they push everything on everyone else. Every question asked to try to get them to acknowledge their part ends up with them pointing the finger at another. The good old blame game. I get it. We all want to be heard and acknowledged but see your part first. What role do you play in the situation? Where can you improve? Do you need to speak up for yourself? Is procrastination your issue? Maybe your communication can stand some improvement.

Next, forgive yourself. We sometimes walk around beating ourselves up for things that happened in our past. Beating up on yourself for things that happened to you or even bad decisions you made is never the answer. Look to learn from your mistakes. What was your reasoning for making those choices at that time? Own it and move forward.

AFFIRMATION

I am the creation of the Most High.
I am made in the image of the King.
I am an original creation from head to toe.
I serve a purpose in this world.
I am valuable.
I release hesitation and make room for victory.

UNLEASH

Recall times in life when you were broken by a person or a circumstance. How did you handle it? What could you have done differently? What needs to change in your life so you become unbreakable?

SOAR

_____

_____

_____

_____

_____

YOUR COMFORT ZONE IS KILLING YOU

As humans we strive to be comfortable. We like things just the way we like them and when our conditions aren't met there is usually a problem. For instance, when you get home from work one of the first things you probably do is notice the temperature of your house and adjust the thermostat. If it's too cold, it's a problem. If it's too hot, it's a problem. Most of us cannot function properly if our surroundings are out of sort, so we go about life making sure all conditions are favorable and we have a level of comfort.

Can I propose to you that it is good to be uncomfortable? Yes. It is *good* to be uncomfortable. I've never met anyone who was destined for greatness that achieved it being comfortable. Authors who are submitting their final copy of their book are uncomfortable. Pregnant women in their final trimester are uncomfortable. People with a huge purpose trapped inside of them are uncomfortable. We've been conditioned to making sure that we're comfortable as we move through life. I want to suggest that you get used to being uncomfortable if you want to live a life of purpose.

I don't know if you've noticed it or not but your comfort zone is killing you. That space in life that you've taken so much time creating so that things aren't topsy turvy, out of sorts and uncomfortable is your comfort zone. It's the zone you retreat to that makes it okay to *not* start the business, *not* answer the call of ministry, **not** write the book and **not** become an international speaker. When you abide in that zone you are safe from added responsibility, being stretched, and failure. What you do not realize is that while you hang out in your comfort zone you also rob yourself of victories, mountaintop experiences and the feeling of success.

Your purpose has already been established. God chose it before you arrived. As a matter of fact, it's the very reason you are here on earth. Can I tell you that you'll never fulfill your purpose dwelling inside your comfort zone? Your place of purpose and your comfort zone are longtime enemies. They hate each other with a passion and they will do all they can to pull you to their side. You can either let your comfort zone kill your dreams, passions, and desires for a better life or you can be determined to pack your bags and move out of your comfort zone for good. The latter will make your life so much better.

I am no longer living in my comfort zone.
I am comfortable being uncomfortable.

UNLEASH

What does your comfort zone look like? How much time have you wasted creating it? What steps will you take to pack up and move out of your comfort zone so you can pursue your purpose?

SOAR

_____

_____

_____

_____

_____

DON'T TAKE IT PERSONALLY

From time to time, most of us find ourselves offended by something someone said, or perhaps did to us. You don't get invited to a party that everyone else you know is going to.

Your boss praises your coworker in the company meeting, but doesn't acknowledge any of your efforts. You don't receive a thank you card for the birthday gift you gave someone. Your son sits out on the bench the entire baseball game, while the coach's son and his circle of friends play the whole time. It can be so difficult to overlook these kinds of annoyances.

Some people aren't confrontational, but may get just as offended. Rather than pick a fight with the offender, they stew about what the person said or did, harboring all kinds of negative emotions. These kinds of feelings can fester and turn someone into an angry, bitter, miserable person. It can also lead to grudges. I know people who have spent years estranged from close friends over relatively small offenses.

Let's be real … offenses are going to come your way. When they do it is okay to admit that it hurt but you shouldn't get upset about it. You can choose to not be offended because the Bible says we should be *"bearing with one another, if anyone has a complaint against another; even as Christ forgave you, so you also must do."*

Why are some people so brash with others? I believe it's because hurt people hurt people. When life gets tough for some they lash out at the closest person to them and that could be you. So, what do you do when you're faced with the lash out or hurtful words and actions of others? Don't take it personally. Take the background and experiences of others into account. We all have different upbringings, pasts and cultures.

If anger rises because of the actions or words of another I suggest you deal with it quickly. Anger is a necessary emotion. Even the Bible tells us to be angry and sin not. Many people haven't been taught how to deal with anger.

Those who lack self-control
 usually allow their anger to explode into fits of rage which can include spewing hurtful language. If you are on the receiving end, don't take it personally. I know it's easier said than done but you must not allow someone else's lack of self-control to allow you to act out of character. Forgiveness is mandatory if you want to live boldly and beyond limits.

Next time you find yourself getting offended, pause and think things through. You may realize it's not something to get upset about. Remember, we all have unique personalities. Allow for those differences, ignore the unpleasant mistakes, and learn to enjoy other people.

I let go of my anger so I can see clearly.
I am courageous and I stand up for myself.
My life and health are more important than strife and
misunderstandings.

UNLEASH

When was the last time you allowed yourself to be offended?
Have you unnecessarily held on to negative emotions
towards someone? Do you need to address the person or talk
it out in a mirror with your reflection? Find a new way of
handling offenses by coming up a blanket response to use
whenever you are offended.

SOAR

_____

_____

_____

_____

_____

TAKE THE RAW STUFF

I once heard Bishop TD Jakes say, *"God gives you the raw stuff to give you something to think about, so you can ask what can I do with the stuff you gave me?"* Please allow me to be honest. I'm guilty of God giving me *'raw stuff'* my entire life and sometimes I complained asking for finished products instead.

God promoted me to Director of a dance ministry at a mega church when I was in my late 20's. The ministry looked like *'raw stuff'* because everything needed an overhaul: the structure, the garments, the dancers' skill level, the syllabus. I remember asking God why couldn't He give me a ministry to lead that was top notch and ready to roll. That would be so much fun! Why did I have to start from scratch? He later showed me that those seven years I spent serving as their leader taught me firsthand about my leadership ability and style, my relationship with God, how to build healthy relationships with others, how to recognize potential in others, how to groom next level leaders and so much more.

God used the *'raw stuff'* as the foundation for my coaching firm and that experience was vital in me becoming the Confidence Coach I am today. I also learned to 'never despise small beginnings' because they just may be the thing God has chosen to bring out the best and the next best thing in *me*.

How do you view the *'raw stuff'* that is in front of you?

I embrace small beginnings.
I realize that God is using what is in my hands to build what is next for me.

UNLEASH

Are you guilty of looking at the 'raw stuff' as just stuff and discarding it? Have you embraced the puzzle pieces and worked diligently to make a beautiful picture or are you frustrated with the number of small pieces you have and leave them disjointed? Find a new way looking at the 'raw stuff' in your life.

SOAR

_____

_____

_____

_____

_____

JUST SAY IT

Julie is one of the nicest people I know. She's always been the person to choose silence over confrontation. She adopted the mindset of "just let it go" early in life. Julie hates confrontation and avoids it at all costs but the older she got she realized that silence can be deadly. Julie's husband is overbearing and he questions every move she makes and frequently accuses her of being unfaithful. His paranoia doesn't sit well with Julie but she never says anything to him about it for fear of confrontation. Simple conversations turn into shouting matches quickly and it upsets Julie. She was raised in a quiet household where shouting was never an option. Her husband came from a loud, outspoken family when a raised voice was the only way to be heard. After eight years of marriage Julie began to experience chest pains. She soon realized that holding in her feelings and especially her anger was affecting her health.

Can you relate to Julie's story at all? Julie finally realized that her needs were important and so was her health. If she wanted to start living a great life, she must start living it "off the wall" as Michael Jackson put it. This means she had to make her own choices and voice them.

Making the change to speak up may not be easy. People may resist the new you, especially those who benefited from you keeping quiet and going along with the flow. There is a certain freedom that comes with respectfully letting your voice be heard. Talk Show Host Wendy Williams has a jingle that begins with "say it like you mean it" and if you want to live boldly and beyond limits that's exactly what you must learn to do.

The nice southern girl in me says "say it with a smile and never be disrespectful." The Christian in me says "say everything in love." The 40-year old liberated me says "whatever you do, just say it!"

AFFIRMATION

I am too big of a gift to the world to silence my voice.
I have a voice and I deserve to be heard.
I am enough.

UNLEASH

Release the idea of holding your thoughts and comments inside and recognize the fact that your words matter. Your opinions count. Your voice deserves to be heard loud and clear.

SOAR

_____

_____

_____

_____

_____

_____

WE'VE BEEN WAITING ON YOU

Stop waiting for SOMEONE ELSE to do it.
YOU DO IT.
Stop waiting for SOMEONE ELSE to go first.
YOU GO FIRST.
Stop waiting for SOMEONE ELSE to make a difference.
YOU MAKE A DIFFERENCE.

Have you ever heard anyone say, '*if something really bothers you then you just may be the person to fix it*'? It is true. Many of us spend far too much time complaining about how things out to be or the fact that no one is doing anything about an issue we see. In those instances, we are waiting for someone else to be the answer, to solve the problem and to make a difference.

God often gives us a burden not so we can complain and constantly point it out but so we will be moved to produce the solution.

AFFIRMATION

Everything I need is already inside of me.
I hold the answer to someone's problem.
I am enough.

UNLEASH

Refuse to continue complaining but replace it with some
serious thought. How can YOU be the answer to the
problems you see before you?

SOAR

_____

_____

_____

_____

_____

_____

GET RID OF IT

If you're like me you do not mind getting rid of things. Nothing bothers me more than a cluttered desk, a junky closet or an unorganized kitchen cabinet. Disorganization affects my ability to think clearly so before I can start my day everything must be in its place. It is easy to visually identify areas of my office or home that may need to be purged but what about my emotions? Often, we walk around carrying a lot of unnecessary emotional baggage from our past such as hurt, disappointment and rejection. Those are real emotions and I've learned that you can't just suppress them. If you continue to push them down inside and pile more on top of them these bottled up emotions will manifest in other areas such as weight gain, stress, drinking, drugs, depression … the list goes on. Release it.

You can.

AFFIRMATION

I let go of the past so I can grow.
I turn negatives into positives.
I welcome positive energy to live my life to the fullest.

UNLEASH

Imagine you could bottle up all the negativity, issues, hurt and pain you carry inside and blow it into a balloon, tie the end tight and release it in an open field. As you stand there watching it float away you feel the negativity leave your body. Visualizing this process may work or you may have to take a trip to an open field, a parking lot or your backyard to release a balloon along with all you've carried inside. You deserve to live beyond limits so release the things that have held you captive.

SOAR

_____

_____

_____

_____

_____

DESTROY THAT BOX

I recently attended an event held at my high school and had a conversation with a classmate I hadn't seen in about 12 years. He asked what I did for a living. After telling him about my dance-based fitness company and nonprofit organization for women he responded by saying, "I always knew you would be successful because you were always different." I said, "Different?" He said, "Yeah, different in an effective way. You didn't do things like everyone else. You weren't afraid to do things no one else was doing. Different."

As kids in elementary school all we want to do is fit in. To solidify this point even further, my little girl came home from pre-school asking for ribbons in her hair because her friend in class wore them. Your kids may ask for the latest video game, clothes or even cell phone because fitting in means they're viewed as being cool. Young adults seek status and approval by keeping up with the hottest fashion and using the latest slang. Adults purchase homes in the finest neighborhoods and drive certain types of cars all so they can fit in with the crowd that is accepted. For most people, fitting in is a way of life and standing out or going against the grain is simply not an option.

I've discovered to live boldly and beyond limits you must embrace your uniqueness and stand out. After being conditioned to fit in, it can be challenging to change our way of thinking once you realize the intention has always been to stand out.

In whatever field you are in someone came before you and created a box or one set way of doing things and it has probably been adopted by others as the "norm". My question is what does that all must do with you? If you've been operating in a box created by you or anyone else don't just step outside of it but destroy it.

You've heard the term "*think outside of the box.*" I challenge you not to only think outside of it but destroy it. You have a path that is unique to you. When you try to run your business, create your brand, manage your kids or even lose weight the way others are doing it you are wasting your time. Embrace what makes you different and destroy that box.

AFFIRMATION

I trust my inner wisdom and intuition.
Wonderful things are unfolding before me.

UNLEASH

If you've been accustomed to fitting in alter your way of thinking and embrace your originality. Think of ways you can stand out and destroy the box of normalcy!

SOAR

_____

_____

_____

_____

_____

_____

THIS TOO SHALL PASS

Two things are always true. All things have a beginning and an ending. Everything. Think about it. Childhood ends. Seasons end. Assignments end. Even life on earth eventually ends. When you are faced with a particularity tough situation or rough season in life it is very easy to think the tough time will never pass.

Never get comfortable in the struggle. Rocky times whether they be in your relationship, career, finances or health are a mere pass through for something greater. Valleys move you from one mountain to the next and rough seasons take you from one station in life to another. The thing that gets me through rough spots in life is remembering everything has a beginning and an end. In other words, this too shall pass.

I was a major trooper when in labor with my first child if I must say so myself. I'll be honest with you, when I found out I was pregnant with my son the thought of labor frightened me. I heard everyone's horror stories and the images I conjured up in my mind were horrific! I was having my first child, so I didn't know what to expect, but I held on to the idea of labor having a beginning and an end. My water broke in bed one Sunday evening at 11:30pm and it was on! I got up from bed, washed a load of clothes, and ran a bath, read a few books all while stopping to breathe each time; suddenly a rushing wave otherwise known as a contraction hit my body. I'd read all the books that were available to me over the past eight months and now the moment of truth was here. Because I was armed with knowledge I knew I could physically and mentally get through labor. With each passing minute and painful contraction, I knew I was closer to it being over. I logged the length of each contraction and kept a level head. At 8:08am on a warm September morning I welcomed Zamar to the world with a smile and an "I love you." It was over!

You may not physically be in labor right now but you probably are in a situation or place in life where something needs to end. Have you heard the phrase "it's always darkest before dawn"? It exists so we will know there is hope even in the worst of circumstances. It can be difficult to see just how close we are to our next mountain top moment when we have our heads down drugging forward. There is solace in knowing that with every step we take forward we are closer to the top of that mountain and victory is closer than it was before.

AFFIRMATION

Everything happening now is happening for my ultimate good.

My ability to conquer my challenges is limitless; my potential to succeed is infinite.

I grow in strength with every forward step I take.

UNLEASH

Let go of the need to rush through tough situations in life or the urge to give up during trials. Unleash your inner survivor and make it to the mountain top!

SOAR

_____

_____

_____

_____

_____

_____

OPPOSITION

Opposition: resistance; the condition of being in conflict; something that serves as an obstacle; a position facing an opposite another.

Why does opposition exist? Opposition exists to keep you from moving forward. Period! Opposition appears in the form of: lack of money, not enough time, closed doors, negative thoughts, and fear of failure. We all face opposition in life but how do we handle it? Some people see opposition as a reason to quit. Your complications are not an indication that you will not reach your goal. If you truly desire success you must learn to overcome oppositions without giving up. Orison Swett Marden said, *"Success is not measured by what you accomplish, but by the opposition you have encountered, and the courage with which you have maintained the struggle against overwhelming odds."* How can you live through the struggle?

DO NOT FOCUS ON THE OPPOSING FORCE
Remember, what you focus on only magnifies! If you spend your precious time (because we can never get it back) with your eyes focused on opposition it will cause fear, frustration and feelings of defeat. Too many times people entertain defeat when they haven't taken the first step. Now I believe its one thing to feel defeated after you've put forth an effort but why or why should you feel defeat when you're still sitting at the starting line? Not acceptable my friend. Keep your eyes on what you want to magnify.

VISUALIZE YOUR ENDING

Look past the opposition and see your desired result. Is it a successful business? Is it a loving, peaceful marriage? Is it a thriving ministry? See the end and keep your eyes fixed on it. I know it's tough to look past debt when bills are constantly coming in but find a way to see your financial freedom until it manifests. Your sight will help guide your choices, actions and words. Soon you'll be making decisions based on what you want to see come to fruition in your life opposed to the chaos that may be going on right now.

AFFIRMATION

I am moving closer to my goals with each step.
I believe things are getting better each day.
I see my path getting clearer each day.

UNLEASH

You have the power through visualization to see the thing
you desire. Continue to keep your eyes fixed on it until it is
your reality. Unleash a laser-focused vision and see your
way through opposition.

SOAR

_____

_____

_____

_____

_____

PERCEPTION IS EVERYTHING

Transition. You can either welcome it or fight against it. Transitions are bridges that connect what we've become accustomed to and the unknown. Life as you know it changes. Your surroundings are unfamiliar and that's extremely uncomfortable. I've found that we run fast and hard from being comfortable. We like the predictability of life. Routines give us comfort and that's normal but what happens when transitions appear? Will you see it as the end or the beginning?

I'll use a seed to help you understand. A person takes a seed and plants it in the ground. The seed must be pushed deep into the soil to grow. It's undetected and is out of sight. It is hidden. What looks like death is actually a birthing process in its early stages. What seems like isolation is really incubation. What feels like abandonment is tender loving care. When the seed is watered while it is protected by the soil it begins to burst and everything on the inside pushes past its shell as it attaches itself to the soil. Roots grow deep providing the soon to be plant with a firm foundation. The plant pushes against the heavy soil and eventually breaks forth above the ground in search of light. Now that the life cycle of being beneath the soil is complete the plant begins another phase of expanding, budding and blooming. Others begin to admire the strength and beauty of the plant which once started out as a seed.

Now, let's take a look at the process of the seed and see where you fit. God has placed everything you need inside of you. In order to bring the best of you out it may require you to be pushed deep into soil or situations to grow. Your greatness goes undetected because you are hidden and what looks like it's killing you is actually the birthing process of what's always been inside of you. What feels like isolation is really the place where your greatness is being cultivated. Ideas, dreams, businesses, books and everything else that's been inside you pushes past the shell of doubt and begins to grow. Your planning and preparation serve as roots that create a firm foundation. Above ground everyone can see your dreams begin to blossom. So, is what you're going through right now killing you or making you into something brand new? Better? Stronger? Greater? Perception is everything.

AFFIRMATION

I choose to see the good in life.
I am in charge of my thoughts and I think good thoughts.
Every positive action I take leads to greater
accomplishments.

UNLEASH

Take a moment and look at some setbacks that came in life
through different eyes. How did the past hurts actually help
you along your journey?

SOAR

_____

_____

_____

_____

_____

_____

DREAM AGAIN

I really hope you have not stopped dreaming. I recently asked my son what he wants to be when he grows up. I ask him periodically because at that age ambitions seem to change weekly. He usually gives me at least five professions and I look for ways to encourage him and drive his interests in the right direction. Do you remember those days? The days when you were a kid and had lofty ambitions of being a teacher, fireman, lawyer, WWE wrestler AND chef? Now that you're an adult it may be tough visualizing just one dream.

I recently held a coaching session with a wonderful young lady who is a single parent and had a lot on her plate. Just sitting and listening to her schedule made me exhausted. I asked her what her life looked like five years from now. Silence fell on the telephone line. She finally spoke and told me she had no clue. She knew what she absolutely had to get done that week but she did not know what life would look like in the future. Now I realize that none of us are fortune tellers, but how can we press toward the mark if we have no idea of what that mark looks like? As she spoke, I sat in my office chair and wrote down two words. Dream again.

Dream again and get a picture in your mind of what success looks like for you. No matter which way the wind blows your life never allow it to blow your dreams out of view. When our plates are full it's very easy to put our head down and get consumed in the grind, the hustle, the digging ourselves out of financial debt, a breakup or divorce or whatever the situation. In the midst of surviving, our dreams sometimes turn into a vapor and slowly fade away. Before you know if you've lifted your head only to realize you've been left with the grind.

I challenge you to walk away from the hustle for a moment and search for your dream. Visualize it. When the plowing is all said and done what do your crops look like? A farmer tills soil preparing his land for the seeds he's going to plant. As he plants and waters I bet he looks up occasionally and sees the field full of the harvest he is expecting. We should do the same. What is all the grinding for? What are the sleepless nights and tears for? Visualize your dream. See it and continue to see it until you can make out all the details. It may not materialize exactly as your mind's eye sees it but at least you're dreaming again.

AFFIRMATION

I take risks and try new things without fear.
I am motivated to continue pursuing my goals.
I feel alive, energized and motivated to dream again.

UNLEASH

Shake off anything that holds you down and dare to dream
again. Pull out a notebook and write down your heart's
desire. Refuse to allow negative thoughts to creep in. Write
freely as if time or money doesn't matter. Dream again.

SOAR

_____

_____

_____

_____

_____

IT'S ALREADY IN YOU

I've been blessed with many gifts and dance happens to be one of them. I've had the privilege of performing in many venues before thousands of people. The most emotional experience had to be the African American Cultural Festival in Raleigh, NC in 2013. The crowd was about 30,000 and the weather was great! I was up next to teach a line dancing segment. It's easy to get a crowd moving and engaged when you are a singer or hip hop artist but when you are a fitness instructor it gets a little tricky. To engage a large audience of people and have everyone moving in unison takes skill and charisma. I have them both.

Stage performances and charisma is something I learned from my father. Bill Moore was a quartet singer. He knew how to engage an audience from the time he hit the platform until he put his microphone in the stand and walked off. I sat in church and watched him thousands of time over the course of my life and was always amazed at how easy he made it look. Not everyone knew how to do that, but later in life I realized I did.

As I walked to take the stage for my Line Dance N2 Shape segment at the festival I started thinking about my dad who had died 10 years prior. I thought about how proud he would be to see his little girl do what he'd done so many times before … connect with people and make them smile. Tears began to run down my eyes as I thought of how he's passed on what brought him so much joy. Now when I grace any stage - small or large – whether I'm dancing or speaking I reassure myself that this is what I was born to do and "it's in me."

What's in you?

AFFIRMATION

I have everything in me to succeed in life.
I am already awesome.
I am enough just as I am.

UNLEASH

The thing you are built to do is already in you. There's a reason you are drawn to it like a magnet. Take some time and identify dreams that have been lying dormant for some time.

SOAR

_____

_____

_____

_____

_____

_____

TIME KEEPS ON TICKING

Many people are so stuck in their past that God could drop a new life on top of them and they'd instantly fill it with their past life.

Stuck: baffled caught or fixed, full of difficulty or confusion or bewilderment.

Time stands still for no one. Let me ask you a question. Is your past worth replaying? If not, it's time to start living in the moment. It happened. He left you. You were overlooked for the promotion. Your business idea didn't work the first time. When my friends come to me with their problems I tell them you have two choices. You can stay right where you are or you can move forward. Yes, everyone wants to move forward but continuing to discuss and re-live a situation is not moving forward. Just as the hands on the clock continue to tick in a forward motion so should you. The second hand moves faster than the minute and hour hands and sometimes in life we should move forward at a nice steady pace. When God gives you a business idea there's no need to wait 10 years to move on it. Perfection is a form of fear. If you are waiting until all the pieces line up perfectly you are really afraid of moving at all. Be careful that you don't give way to fear and describe it as being cautious. If you feel the time is now make forward progress in bringing it into fruition. Now I'm not saying if you get a business idea on Monday you should quit your full-time job on Wednesday. Instead, make steady forward progress and you will eventually live that which God once caused you to see. Time keeps moving forward and so should you if you're ever going to meet up with your destiny.

AFFIRMATION

I respect time and it works for me.
I am committed to completing my goals in a timely manner.
I use my time wisely always.

UNLEASH

Eliminate all time snatchers in your life. Time snatchers are
trivial things that eat away at your time (personal phone calls,
texting, surfing the web, going through email, etc.). Set aside
time specifically for time snatchers with the goal of being
more productive.

SOAR

_____

_____

_____

_____

_____

RELAX

Things aren't going just the way you would like them. You are looking to be on top and things just aren't panning out the way you thought they would. There is a scripture that reads, "for we walk by faith, not by sight." We shouldn't focus so much on our current set of circumstances. How do you do that? The things in front of you are screaming FOCUS ON ME, FOCUS ON ME! So, what should you do?

Relax.

One thing I know for sure is that everything has an end and that includes whatever you are going through. Know that your present set of circumstances will not last forever, so take a moment and relax. I know what it is to be in tough situations and someone looks at you and says, "Just relax." You want to grab them by the shoulders and explain the intensity of your struggle and maybe then they will understand the need for your anxiety. I want you to know that if you are still breathing it isn't too late to get a handle on things and you must begin by relaxing.

I am amazed by people on my Facebook timeline that are always going, going, going. They are constantly burning the midnight oil, staying up all night, working on a few hours of sleep. I believe it's called "the grind". Their life seems to be lived in the express lane 24/7. Go! Go! Go! There may be a need to push hard every now and then to meet a deadline for a project, but I question those who think they don't need to relax. Relaxing isn't for wimps and is not synonymous with laziness. We all need to learn to relax.

I know a woman named Gloria. She has a go, go, go personality. She works in ministry and believes if she isn't constantly working and working hard she isn't pulling her weight. Gloria has a habit of putting the weight of the entire ministry on her shoulders even where there are those around her waiting to help her. How many people know that if Gloria does not take some time to unplug from ministry and relax she won't be whole enough to effectively minister to God has assigned her to or enjoy her life?

Take a moment right now and steal some time to relax. Close your eyes and concentrate on your breathing. Inhale through your nose and exhale through your nose. Imagine a field of flowers and a gentle breeze as the sun beams on your face. As you exhale feel your muscles melt. Release any tension you feel in any parts of your body: your face, your shoulders, your back. As you inhale think RE and as you exhale think LAX. Re-Lax. Re-Lax. Re-Lax. As you open your eyes notice how your mind and body feel. You should feel refreshed. Do yourself a favor and find at least three times a day for your new relaxation exercise.

AFFIRMATION

I embrace the peace and quiet of this very moment.
I flow with the wave of life.
(inhale) Re (exhale) LAAAXXXXXX

UNLEASH

Whenever you are stressed take time out for the relaxation exercise.

SOAR

_____

_____

_____

_____

_____

STAND

Life can really beat you down. There are ebbs and flows, ups and downs, peaks and valleys. In those valleys it can be tough to get a handle on things and life is like a sweater with one loose thread and once you pull it everything becomes unraveled. So, what do you do when the bottom falls out? It's simple. You stand.

Ephesians 6:13

Stand: to be in an upright position with all your weight on your feet; support yourself on the feet in an erect position; to rise to an erect position; maintain one's position; to endure successfully; remain firm.

Order in life is a must. When things are out of order getting them back in order may be uncomfortable but it's necessary. The first thing we must do is stand. As you can see from the definition of the word, standing isn't as passive as a position as you may think. Look at words like support yourself, endure, rise and remain firm. Those words sound pretty powerful to me!

It's a natural tendency to desire support from others when times are tough. Even if we don't like their advice, just hearing someone tell us how much they believe in us is comforting. So, what happens when you're in the midst of turmoil and your phone doesn't ring? Instead of checking on you your friends may be chatting amongst themselves about how you ended up where you are or in the mess you're in. This can be very disheartening, especially if you are the friend that always encourages everyone else.

Your circle may be reaching out to you but you may be the type of person that prefers to go through things alone. Some of us just don't want others in our business. Understandable. Whatever the case may be, you still need support, so support YOURSELF.

Remember, standing requires that you support you. How do you do that? Well, would you support your best friend if they were in your shoes right now? Would you pray for them? Would you treat them to an evening out? Share some encouraging words? Those are all the things you should begin to do for yourself. Start today. Pull out that journal you never used or stop by Target and get a good old notebook. Begin and end each day with an encouraging note to yourself. When you start feeling down, read what you've written. You're great at encouraging others. Now it's time to stand and support yourself.

AFFIRMATION

I am strong enough to stand during any situation.
I am built to last.
I am victorious.

UNLEASH

Read over the definition of 'stand' and identify ways you can stand during your tests.

SOAR

_____

_____

_____

_____

_____

_____

REMAIN FLEXIBLE

We set plans and courses for our lives all the time. You can be super deep and spiritual and say you don't but I'll bet you have a general overview of what the next five or 10 years of your life will look like. You probably have planned your vacations, holidays and family time all mapped out. Entrepreneurs have created their marketing plans, projections and programs for the year. We've been taught since childhood to plan ahead. A quote I love is "if you fail to plan you plan to fail."

What happens when you are so married to your plan that you aren't open to any other possibilities? You just may miss a golden opportunity. See, opportunities don't always appear in nice, pretty boxes with lovely ribbons tied to the top. As a matter of fact they never do. It could come in the disguise of hard work or could even feel like a setback. The key is to remain flexible and not so rigid. Be willing to bend so you don't break.

AFFIRMATION

I am unbreakable.

I have the ability to change courses without giving up.

I have great potential and I plan to use it.

UNLEASH

No matter how tight the plan you should always leave room for change. How do you react when there is a sudden change in plans? Is it positive or negative? Resist the need to fight change and figure out how you can be more flexible.

SOAR

_____

_____

_____

_____

_____

_____

MOVE SOMETHING

Most people fill their schedules with all types of things and very seldom find the time for physical exercise. Exercise should be near the top of our daily To Do list right near prayer, planning and breathing. Too often those seeking success burn the candle at both ends rising early and working late all week. If most people knew the benefits exercise they would possibly place it on their schedule on a regular basis.

Whenever you need a boost of energy instead of reaching for a quick caffeine fix, try exercise. Physical activity delivers oxygen and nutrients to your tissues and helps your cardiovascular system work more efficiently. When your heart and lungs function properly you have more energy to go about your daily chores.

Do you need to improve your mood? Try exercise. We all have stressful days and instead of a glass of wine or a bowl of mac and cheese, try exercise. After a workout your brain chemicals are stimulated leaving you feeling happier and more relaxed. Plan a brisk walk immediately after a stressful meeting and see how much better you'll feel afterwards.

What I want you to realize is that exercise is the answer for many of your issues. Its purpose goes deeper than trying to get into a wedding dress or shed a few pounds before a class reunion. Our bodies were designed to move, but most of us lack motivation.

The key to staying motivated to exercise on a regular basis is simple. Get clear on the benefits of physical activity and come to the realization that it is not an option. If you are seeking to live a long, prosperous life exercise is essential. Find a physical activity that you enjoy. It's the best way to make exercise a part of your life instead of a laborious chore. Jogging, dancing, tennis, roller skating and swimming are good forms of exercise. Vow to make physical activity a regular part of your day and watch your mood, health and life improve.

AFFIRMATION

My health is important to me.
I love my body and I choose to treat it well.
My body is a temple and I treat it as such.
I feed my body only what is good for it.
I am a good steward over the body I've been given.

UNLEASH

Upgrade your thinking as it relates to physical activity. Open your mind to see the need for regular physical activity. Create a fitness plan for the week, find an accountability partner and stick to it.

SOAR

_____

_____

_____

_____

_____

_____

CLOSE THE DOOR BEHIND YOU

Rough patches. We all hit them in life. Marriages have ups and downs. Kids go through stages of disobedience trying to find their way. Work can be demanding and downright draining. I've had my share of rough patches. Divorce. Moving. Feelings of abandonment. Let me tell you, if you're not careful you can get a little too comfortable with the struggle. My friend, I don't ever want you to get used to the struggle. Never set up shop in the midst of trouble. I don't care if your relationship has hit some turbulence. Refuse to give up and stay in your present set of circumstances. Things can get better. They will get better. They must get better, but they won't if you give up where you are.

When will you make the decision to walk away from what you are experiencing so better can enter your life? Quit accepting mediocre when you were made for excellence!

AFFIRMATION

I no longer focus on my past.
I move forward daily.
What's ahead of me is brighter than what's behind me.

UNLEASH

How can you free yourself from your past struggles? Are you still holding on to some aspects of the struggle? Elaborate below.

SOAR

_____

_____

_____

_____

_____

_____

TAKE CONTROL OF YOUR LIFE

Give yourself permission to live the life you want. It does not matter who agrees or disagrees. The only person you need to please is the person staring back at you in the mirror. There is no rule that says your decisions must be approved by others in your life. Your friends and family may weigh in on some decisions you make but you and only have the deciding vote. If you have gotten used to relying on external validation like praise from other people to feel good about yourself you're going to have to make a change. Confidence is key and those who truly believe in themselves find peace within instead of seeking validation from others.

When you take control of your life you not only feel more confident but you also take back your power. It feels good to make decisions, especially when they lead to success. You will naturally feel like you deserve more in life. Once you come to the realization that you deserve more, you will achieve more. It is a beautiful cycle.

AFFIRMATION

I feel motivated and am moving in the direction of my dreams.
I trust my thought process.
I enjoy being responsible for my actions.

UNLEASH

Life consists of each day, not just the big events sometime in the future. Don't forget to take responsibility for the little things today. Do not postpone it. Taking responsibility for your life is not something you master over the weekend. Get started today.

SOAR

_____

_____

_____

YOU ARE AN ORIGINAL.
STOP FIGHTING IT.

Why do we shy away from being original? As little kids we try our hardest to fit in with others in school.
We quickly learned as kids that standing out will get you picked on and isolated. As we've gotten older we learned that each of us is an ORIGINAL with a unique purpose and instead of FITTING IN we should be STANDING OUT. It is our originality that sets us apart from the pack and allows our inner light to SHINE and bless others.

Stop dimming your light.
Get comfortable in your skin.
Bask in your originality!
YOU have something to offer the world and it's found in your ORIGINALITY!

AFFIRMATION

I am unique.
I embrace my individuality.
I enjoy being different.

UNLEASH

There is no one else quite like you, so stop seeking to fit in when you do not. Understand that standing out is what you were created to do. Look for opportunities to stand out this week and embrace them.

SOAR

_____

_____

_____

TRUST IN GOD

God wants us to put Him first in our lives. He wants us to put our confidence and trust in Him, all the time, in everything. When you learn to do that you will truly begin to unleash and soar!

AFFIRMATION

I trust God.
I allow God to lead my life.
I am obedient to the voice of God.

UNLEASH

How can you begin to trust, lean and depend on God more today?

SOAR

_____

_____

_____

ACKNOWLEDGEMENTS

With special thanks:

- ❖ To my husband David Brown, II for all your love and support. You are my biggest cheerleader. Without your motivation and encouragement, this book might never have been written. Thank you for continuing to push me out of my comfort zone.

- ❖ To my son Zamar and daughter Gracen who are just as proud of me as I am of them. Thanks for being my *"mac and cheese"*.

- ❖ To my sister Robin Bridges who infected me with the reading bug as a child. Thanks for all those trips to the library, sis. They paid off!

- ❖ To my prayer partner Michelle Dawson who has never judged me but always agreed with me in prayer for my projects, my family and my destiny. Thank you from the bottom of my heart.

- ❖ To the late Mrs. Dorothy Phelps-Jones of Reidsville, NC who encouraged and inspired me as a young girl to shine no matter what.

- ❖ To my friends Valerie Cogdell Jamieson, Leslie Courts, Meloney Miller, Sharon Fryar, and Emelia

Cowans for supporting me, loving me and being true friends.

ABOUT THE AUTHOR

Witty, caring, motivating and inspiring are just a few words that describe Tina Moore Brown. Known for her energetic personality and sense of humor she somehow makes embracing one's greatness possible. She wears many hats and improves the lives of others in several different ways. Her  Confidence is Key coaching sessions inspire people to believe in themselves again. Her workout programs motivate women to be fit. Tina's passion is to inspire people to live healthy, happy and whole lives and she's making a difference one person at a time!

Tina is a wife, mother, entrepreneur, author, motivational speaker, confidence coach, leadership trainer, fitness instructor, and motivational speaker.

None of her accomplishments would be possible without the love and support of her husband, David H. Brown, II. They are one in marriage and in business and provide a loving home for their children: Zamar & Gracen.

Contact Tina at **www.TinaMooreBrown.com** or feel free to email her at **TMB@TinaMooreBrown.com**.

Also by Tina Moore Brown

From Dream to Destiny: Unlocking the Winner, Champion, and Finisher Within

Soon to be Released by Tina Moore Brown

You Were Made to Shine

The Fight for Freedom

Made in the USA
Monee, IL
23 June 2021

72138062R00055